BODY
dynamics

The Ultimate Women's
Workout Book

Nikki Diamond & Carolyn Cheshire

WARD LOCK

A WARD LOCK BOOK

First published in the UK 1996
by Ward Lock
Wellington House
125 Strand
LONDON
WC2R OBB

A Cassell Imprint

Distributed in the United States
by Sterling Publishing Co., Inc.
387 Park Avenue South, New York, NT 10016-8810

A British Library Cataloguing in Publication Data block for this book may be obtained from the British Library.

ISBN 0 7063 7537 8

Designed by Grahame Dudley Associates

Printed and bound in Great Britain by The Bath Press, Avon

The information contained in this book is intended to serve as a guide for those who wish to use weights as a part of their training programme. It is not intended to be a substitute for professional medical advice or training. The authors and publishers disclaim any responsibility or liability for any loss or damage that may occur as a result of information, procedures, or techniques included in this work. Before beginning this, or any other, exercise programme, it is advisable to obtain the approval and recommendation of your physician.

Contents

The Authors

Carolyn Cheshire's name is synonymous with weight training. She was the first professional female bodybuilder in the UK, and after becoming British champion went on to compete in the first six 'Miss Olympia' contests in the USA — the most prestigious of all professional bodybuilding contests. She has also competed in the World Women's Championships, World Couples' Championships, and European Championships, with placings in the top three. She has been trained by and learned from some of the most respected names in the world of weight training. For the past ten years Carolyn has been a professional instructor and personal trainer and was voted Britain's best personal trainer. She was also featured in the highly acclaimed movie 'Pumping Iron II: The Women'.

Nikki Diamond is well-known as Scorpio from LWT's popular show 'Gladiators'. From being an inter-school's high jump champion and with a strong background in sprinting and athletics, she went on to compete in major bodybuilding contests before becoming a 'Gladiator'. This requires a tremendous combination of strength, stamina and co-ordination, which Nikki achieves with weight training workouts. She has played a principal role in three pantomines and has co-presented 'On Your Marks', a series of sports programmes for Meridian TV. A role model to her many fans, she is a perfect example of what can be achieved through proper and regular weight training exercise.

Introduction

During the ten years following the publication of Carolyn's book *Body Chic*, there have been countless changes and advances in the fitness industry, some for the better and some not. This is particularly true in the field of weight or resistance training which forms the basis of this book. Today there are more people than ever joining health clubs and gyms and using weights as part of their exercise routine.

Much has also been written on the subject of weight training, some of which can appear confusing, especially to the beginner. Unfortunately a lot of this material centres on the theoretical side which tends to make the subject of weight training both complicated and impractical. It also makes the assumption that we are all exactly the same and that all exercises work equally well for everyone. Experience leads us to believe this is a mistake. We are all individuals with different needs, desires and body types, so using weights is highly individual. That's why there are so many different workout routines. Of course, there are basic weight training exercises which are considered the foundation of weight training and used in most weight training workouts.

Recently there has been a wealth of books and videos promoting the next how-to fitness fad, all claiming that they know the secret of a perfect body with only a few minutes' exercise a day. While a few minutes' exercise a day is certainly better than nothing at all, it will not give you the kind of body you are probably looking for. If it were that easy, everyone would have a body like a supermodel, and there would be no need for any more fitness gurus. It was mainly for this reason, and to address some of the more controversial developments, that we decided to write *Body Dynamics*.

Over the years we have encountered most, if not all, of the problems and uncertainties that you may come across in weight training, and we hope that we have covered as many of the most common ones as possible. We have hopefully exploded some of the many myths and misconceptions surrounding the use of weights and have separated fact from fiction.

This book will not only help you learn everything you need to know before you even go to the gym, but it will also start you off on the right road and help you to get the very best from your workout.

Body Dynamics is written with easy-to-understand photographs taken in an actual gym setting with quick-to-follow instructions, and we have deliberately kept the text to a minimum. Each section is divided into a particular body part for ease of reference. For example, you will find all the exercises for the back under the section for back training regardless of whether you are using machines or free weights or simple free-standing exercises. We have tried to keep this book as practical as possible in the hope that you will use it constantly both in and out of the gym, and with our help achieve the body you have always wanted.

CHAPTER 1

Working Out with Weights

Working out with weights means you can literally change your entire shape by working on specific parts of your body to tone and shape it to get the look you've always wanted. No other form of exercise will tone your muscles in the same way. When you first start, your strength levels will increase rapidly and you can expect to see much firmer and tighter muscles as you progress. If you maintain a consistent approach, you should see results within the first 4-8 weeks.

But having a fit, healthy body does require effort. Nobody was born with the perfect figure. Some may have good genes, which is an advantage, and we all know someone who seems to be able to eat just about anything without adding a single pound in weight. But if, like us, you are one of the remaining 99 per cent of the population who have to work to keep in shape, you will need to work-out regularly to get the results you want. Once you see and feel the benefits, these workouts will become a part of your everyday routine.

Weight training requires a degree of concentration and so going to the gym is also an excellent way to switch off from the day's problems and concentrate on something else — you. Afterwards, your problems might not seem so bad. By joining a gym you are making a commitment and this will help you to stay motivated and achieve your goals. It is probably the best investment of time and money you will ever make.

For a modest outlay you will have access to a place where you can re-shape, tone, trim, and build a healthy body.

Why weights?

It is a fact that from as early as our mid-twenties, our bodies start to deteriorate so that we gradually lose muscle at the rate of approximately 2.3-3.2 kg (5-7 lb) every decade, with joints and bones becoming weaker. Over two million people (mostly women) suffer from osteoporosis (brittle bones) in the UK alone. Using weights as part of your workout will help you to slow this decline and even reverse it. In fact, a controlled weight training programme produces more positive results than most other forms of exercise. Here are just some of the positive health effects of regular weight training, and remember, good health and looking your best go hand in hand.

❶ Avoid muscle loss

Although endurance exercise such as aerobics improves our cardiovascular fitness, it does not prevent the loss of muscle tissue. Only weight training maintains our muscle tone and strength throughout our middle and later life. Our muscle tone keeps us firm and helps us to keep our shape.

❷ Increase bone mineral density

The effects of weight training are similar for bone tissue as for muscle. By increasing bone osteoproteins and mineral content, studies have shown significant increases in bone mineral density, which reduces the risk of osteoporosis.

❸ Reduce body fat

Although a reduction of body fat is a well-known benefit for people who already weight train, recent studies have proved that after just three months on a weight training programme people lost an average 1.8 kg (4 lb) of fat, despite eating more calories per day.

❹ Avoid metabolic rate reduction

Research indicates that the average adult experiences a 2-5 per cent reduction in metabolic rate (the speed at which we burn calories) every decade. Because muscle tissue is an active tissue, it burns calories even at rest. Weight training prevents muscle loss and thereby prevents the accompanying decrease in resting metabolic rate, and the inevitable increase in body fat, more commonly known as middle age spread.

❺ Reduce arthritic pain

Here again, recent studies have concluded that sensible weight training can help to alleviate the pain of osteoarthritis. Most people who suffer from such pain need strength exercises to develop stronger muscles, bone and connective tissue.

Exploding the myths

There are probably more misconceptions and myths surrounding weight training than any other form of sport or exercise. What's even more surprising is that despite the amount of information now being produced, a lot of these misconceptions still exist even today.

Myth 1: Weight training will give me big muscles

This is one of the most widely quoted myths, and the truth of this one is best answered as follows. Someone who plays tennis regularly once or twice a week might get a lot of pleasure and some good exercise, but would hardly consider themselves suitably qualified to enter next year's Wimbledon championships. It's the same with weights — unless you train for six or seven days a week with very heavy weights, follow a strict diet, have the right genes and dedicate your entire life to it, you will not develop a bodybuilder's physique. So it is therefore almost impossible for a woman to develop large muscles, but you will firm and tone your body in a way no other form of exercise can.

Myth 2: My muscle will turn to fat when I stop exercising

Believe it or not, this is a question we are still asked. Muscle and fat are two different tissues. Muscle cannot turn to fat, and fat cannot turn to muscle any more than silver can turn to gold. If you stop exercising, reduce the number of calories you eat accordingly. As you will not be using those extra calories for your weight training, any additional calories will be stored as fat. It's simply a matter of balancing energy (food) intake with energy expenditure (exercise).

Myth 3: It's possible to sweat unwanted fat away

When you perspire heavily in a sauna or plastic wrap you are merely ridding your body of water which will be replaced as soon as you drink fluids.

Myth 4: Squatting will give me a big bottom

It's fat that gives you a big bottom. Squatting exercises, when performed correctly, will firm and tone the largest muscle in the body, your gluteus maximus or bottom.

Myth 5: Weight training will make me muscle bound

This is an often quoted phrase which has been around a long time. The term 'muscle bound' denotes a lack of flexibility. But with weight training it is just the opposite as weight training uses the muscle against a resistance force, and emphasises a complete range of movement with every repetition so there is an improvement in joint and muscle flexibility.

Myth 6: Weight training will slow me down

Weight training is used by athletes in nearly every major sport as part of their training routine. Martina Navratilova, one of the world's greatest tennis stars, recognised the value of weight training to improve her game. Far from slowing her down, it greatly improved her speed.

Myth 7: Weight training will make me lose my bust

This is another old wives' tale often quoted when referring to bench pressing exercises. In fact it is quite the opposite. The pectoral muscles which support and help to keep the bust firm and youthful should be exercised. The bust is made up of fatty tissue, and if you diet you will lose fat from your bust as well as from your waist, hips and bottom.

The bench pressing exercise will help to maintain and support the pectoral muscles around the bust.

Myth 8: No pain, no gain

Weight training should place a demand on the muscle being exercised, but it should NEVER, repeat NEVER, be painful. If any exercise or movement gives you any pain, stop immediately, and try a different exercise. If any pain still exists stop exercising and have the problem checked by a professional.

Myth 9: Weight training is only for the young

As we get older, it becomes even more important to exercise our muscles. Weight training can be started at almost any age. We are always pleased to see older people training in the gyms that we use. Some of them are well into their seventies or even eighties yet are in excellent physical condition — a perfect example to us all that age is certainly no barrier.

Myth 10: Weight training is expensive

For best results join a good gym so you can gain unlimited use of the facilities, can work out, and can meet new friends with similar interests, but most importantly of all keep your body, the only one you will ever have, in the best possible shape.

Myth 11: Weight training is just too complex

There are those who would have you believe that weight training is extremely complex. Our advice is to keep it simple with a few basic exercises which will produce the best results, This is particularly true in the beginning. After a time, try some of the variations as shown in this book.

Myth 12: Weight training will give me huge thighs

The combination of exercise and diet will help remove any excess fat from your legs and the weight training will tone and shape the underlying muscle which will give you those shapely legs you've always wanted.

Myth 13: Pregnant women should not lift weights

It is generally accepted today that pregnant women can continue with their workout routine. Many women find that strong shoulders and chest muscles help support the additional weight of the breasts during pregnancy, and a strong back helps to alleviate lower back pain. Regular exercise improves circulation so if you maintain a well toned body during your pregnancy, you will quickly regain it after birth. Obviously there will be certain exercises you will not be able to perform, such as squats, lunges and leg raises, especially in the later stages of pregnancy when the ligaments soften. Avoid exercises where one hip has to support too much weight as in pregnancy joints are looser and more manoeuvrable. Only do light abdominal exercises and decrease the amount of weight you use. Ask your doctor for advice and listen to your body.

CHAPTER 2

Diet and Nutrition

'Before the war, white bread was one of the most mischievous elements in our national diet, and was responsible for most of the constipation that existed throughout the country. This was because white bread was merely a glutinous substance devoid of vitamins, minerals and roughage.'

This little snippet was taken not from a recent health and fitness magazine publication, but from a copy of *Health & Efficiency* published in 1947. The article went on to explain that white bread was not the only problem, but also pointed out that the national consumption of pastries, packaged foods reduced in vitamins, and heavy meat dishes were also partly to blame. Remember that this particular article was written almost fifty years ago and yet it could easily have come from the latest issue of any health and fitness magazine.

Nutrition is a highly complex subject which is constantly changing. Almost every month new studies are produced which in many cases dismiss the previous thinking on a particular food. One study proclaims we should be eating more of this or that and then a year or so later a second study casts doubt on the theory, dismisses that idea and says we should go back to whatever we were eating before. It all becomes extremely complicated.

So what is the importance of eating correctly?

The human body is the most sophisticated machine on the planet. No other man-made machine comes anywhere near the human body's capabilities, but like machines it needs fuel to run efficiently. Most of us drive a car and use a washing machine, but we would not try to run a car on washing powder or use petrol in the washing machine, or filling either until it's overflowing. It's important to put the right fuel in the right machine. It all seems so obvious when dealing with our cars or washing machines and yet when it comes to the most important machine of all, it all falls apart. Everyday we fill our bodies with all sorts of fuel, the food we eat, sometimes to the point of over-flowing, without any regard to the consequences, until it's too late.

When you begin weight training, you will be using more of the food you eat to cope with the extra energy required for your workouts, so it is important that you develop a sensible eating pattern as well. Before we look at the right kind of food, we should explain what is meant by a sensible eating pattern. No matter what kind of food you are eating, it is generally considered better to eat more smaller meals throughout the day than one or two large ones. This will ensure that you do not over-eat at any one time and removes that over-full feeling when the food seems to take an age to digest, followed by hunger pangs before the next meal arrives. There is no hard and fast rule to this, as factors such as work, time and place, etc. all play a part in how we eat. But, if you can, try to eat more meals but with less food at each meal time.

The importance of a well balanced diet cannot be over emphasised, even more so when you are on a regular exercise programme. Without this, your weight training will not produce the best results. A combination of a nutritious diet and a regular weight training programme is the foundation for a strong, fit and healthy, body. A well balanced diet full of all the right vitamins and minerals can also help to keep you looking younger.

How to plan a balanced diet

With the fast pace of today's lifestyle, it is all too easy to miss meals. Working out during a lunch hour or straight from work can often result in missed meals, even though this is precisely the time you should not miss meals. As no one single food contains all the required nutrients, it is important to eat a variety of foods. Fortunately it is a lot easier today than it was in 1947 to follow a good, sensible eating pattern. Most manufactured foods come in low fat varieties if not zero fat. At last cereal manufacturers are waking up to the demand for cereal products that contain no sugar or salt, and you no longer have to travel miles to find an obscure health food store in order to buy these foods as they are now readily available in nearly every major supermarket. So there really is no excuse for not adopting a healthy eating routine.

Breakfast is the most important meal of the day, and should not be missed. It peps up your metabolism, increases your blood sugar level preventing mid-morning fatigue, and also helps to keep you alert. If you work out at lunchtime make sure to eat a nutritious meal about one hour after your workout. If you work out in the evening, eat a little more during the day and a light meal after your evening workout.

Calories

We have all heard the word 'calorie', but what does it mean in relation to a well-balanced diet? Very simply, a calorie is a unit for measuring the value of foods, and can be divided into three categories: carbohydrates, protein and fat. All food contains either one, two or three of these. If you read the nutritional information on food packets, you will see it written as calories per 100g and per pack. This means the amount of calories divided into carbohydrates, protein and fat, which are found in both 100g and the whole packet.

Carbohydrates

In order to follow a well balanced diet, the main part (approximately 55-60 per cent) of your food intake should come from carbohydrates. This should be made up of foods such as pasta, rice, bread (although not the white stuff mentioned earlier), potatoes and cereals.

Protein

The next most important part of your food intake is protein, and this should make up approximately 20 per cent of your total daily intake. This should come from foods such as meat (preferably white such as chicken because red meat contains high amounts of fat), fish, pulses, nuts and eggs (preferably the white and not the yolk).

Fat

This is the last element in your daily food intake, and here is the problem. Most people eat far more than is required, and fat calories are not always obvious. For example, just a teaspoon of foods like butter, oil and margarine contain approximately 45 calories of pure fat, so it very easy to consume more than is necessary. Fat also contains twice as many calories as carbohydrates and protein, and as the body is very efficient at storing fat, it is extremely important to control the amount of fat intake in your diet, so as stated earlier, read those food labels very carefully, and avoid those products that are high in fat.

Fruit and vegetables

Try to eat at least two to four portions of fruit and three to five portions of vegetables every day. Don't be alarmed by the numbers of portions — a portion is only about a teacup full, so if you have a couple of vegetables with a each meal you will easily consume that amount.

Dairy products

Products such as cheese, milk, yoghurt, etc. are high in animal fat and should be eaten in moderation. Try to find the low fat varieties.

Finally, try to avoid foods like cakes, biscuits, canned drinks, sweets, sugar and salt. They contain virtually no vitamins or minerals and are high in fat and sugar calories. It is generally accepted that too much salt is bad for blood pressure and can be a cause of fluid retention. Remember that we did say having a fit and healthy body required a little effort. But also remember that it doesn't mean giving up entirely on the things you enjoy; it just means cutting down to a sensible level. It's all a question of creating the right balance.

Of course if you starve yourself you will lose weight, but you will also deprive your body of valuable vitamins and minerals. You may also feel miserable existing on a low calorie diet, and you may not have enough energy to continue a regular weight training routine. And as soon as you stop dieting, most of the lost weight always seems to reappear. We find it's far better and much healthier to maintain a sensible eating pattern, with the occasional 'blow-out' meal. During the week be quite strict with your food intake — go for quality, not quantity. At the weekend you can afford to relax a little. Don't worry about the odd piece of cake or ice cream — enjoy it but remember to keep a balance.

Once you have developed a sensible eating pattern, the odd 'big' meal will not make any difference, and you can cut back a little more for a couple of days and put in a extra workout if you are worried.

Vitamin and mineral supplements

There is an awful lot of talk today about the value or otherwise of extra vitamin and mineral supplements. Some studies claim there is a value, while others claim that we get all the vitamins and minerals we need from a well balanced diet. If we could assume that the food we buy has all its vitamin and mineral content and has not lost any through processing or cooking then we would generally agree that we would not need extra supplements. As this is difficult to know, it is probably better to take some form of supplement. We are not suggesting popping handfuls of vitamin tablets every hour, just a simple good quality multivitamin and mineral tablet once a day will be enough.

How much food is enough?

Many women are preoccupied with their weight, but the ratio of body fat to lean muscle is also very important. Two women of the same height of 1.75 m (5 ft 10 in) both weigh 140 lb (10 stone) and both would be considered overweight according to the height/weight charts. One, however, is 140 lb of pure unexercised fat, while the other is a world champion body builder with a body fat ratio in single figures. This illustration shows that weight alone is not the answer. It should be measured with the ratio of body fat to lean muscle.

The question of just how much food we need is complex, and depends largely on age, gender, and lifestyle. As we get older we need fewer calories, so a younger person will require more calories than a mature adult. Women also need fewer calories than men, although if you have an active lifestyle you may need more calories than average. What is clear is that if you know you are carrying excess weight it probably means you are consuming too many calories for your daily needs.

Weight training also plays a part in determining your daily requirements. The most important thing to remember is not to let calorie counting become an obsession. You will be able to see for yourself just by looking in the mirror whether you need to lose a few pounds or not. Be your own judge. But remember, nothing happens overnight, you have to be patient, and as with your weight training, the more you do it the easier it becomes.

When you begin a weight training programme, you will notice changes to your body not only in terms of how it looks on the outside but also with what's happening on the inside. Some people notice that they become more alert, while others report a

THE TEN PRINCIPLES

❶ Try to eat more meals during the day, but with less food.

❷ Get at least half of your daily food intake from carbohydrates.

❸ Get a quarter of your daily food intake from protein.

❹ Get a quarter of your daily food intake from fat.

❺ Avoid foods that are high in fat, sugar and salt.

❻ Eat dairy products in moderation.

❼ Remember that your own daily calorie requirement will depend on factors particular to you.

❽ Eat several portions of fresh fruit and vegetables each day.

❾ Take a multivitamin/mineral supplement each day.

❿ Don't worry about that special occasion meal.

reduction in stress levels and irritability. An increase in appetite is also quite common as you are simply using more calories, and provided you follow the simple nutritional recommendations outlined in this book you should not add any unwanted weight.

As a final point to remember, there are almost as many theories and views on the subject of weight training and nutrition as there are people weight training. Some of these theories or views are passionately held, and you will almost certainly never be short of people who will share their views with you. Try to broaden your understanding and knowledge. Ask questions, read the magazines, but most importantly of all, have fun and enjoy your weight training.

CHAPTER 3

Joining and Using a Gym

The first thing to consider when choosing a gym is convenience. Is the gym near to your place of work or your home? If it is convenient you will be able to make time to go and can establish a routine for yourself more easily. Do you want to exercise during your lunch hour or after work in the evening when you are close to home? After all, you will visiting the place at least two or three times a week, and although the most convenient gym might not be the best equipped, it should be adequate to get you going.

You should also consider the cost. Rather than paying an annual fee all at once, ask if it is possible to pay a monthly membership so you can try out the gym and decide whether it meets your requirements. Just as with any other purchase, it's always a good idea to 'try before you buy' so ask if you can try a session before you sign up for the full membership. There should always be experienced instructors available.

Also, do remember that you don't necessarily have to join a gym — you could easily exercise with free weights at home.

When you first visit a gym, don't be put off by the number of machines and amount of equipment. They can seem quite intimidating at first, but we have trained in countless gyms all over the world and have found every one a welcoming place.

Once you have been training for a few months you should have a good idea of which machine does what and will be able to get around the gym on your own. You can always ask other members for advice and guidance as well as the gym staff. Remember that the person you ask could be in the middle of training, so wait until

Two examples of fixed weight machines.

they finish their set or finish their workout. It's simply good gym etiquette.

Using the equipment

Most gyms will have several types of equipment. Cardiovascular or CV machines for aerobic work include step machines, bikes, treadmills and rowing machines.

There will also be a range of fixed weight machines. Each of these machines is designed to exercise a particular part of the body. The amount of weight is determined by a weight stack fixed to the machine which is adjusted by means of a pin. There are many different makes of these machines on the market, but they all work in much the

Dumb-bell

Barbell

same way and once you have been shown how to use them, you will have no trouble in using any you may come across in another gym.

Some of the better equipped gyms will also have a range of free weights, dumb-bells and barbells. A basic barbell is simply a bar made of steel with weights at either end. A barbell can be either adjustable (the weights at either end can be made heavier or lighter) or fixed. You will usually find a selection of fixed weight barbells in a gym.

The second type of barbell is the Olympic Bar, a steel bar of a standard length and weight which can be 'loaded' to take very heavy weights. It is used for weightlifting and powerlifting sports.

A dumb-bell is simply a shortened version of the barbell. Dumb-bells can also be either adjustable or fixed. You will also find a range of dumb-bells in your gym. They will be in pairs and will progress in intervals from very light weights to very heavy weights.

Free weights are always better as they do not restrict movement and so give greater scope in the exercise. Free weights do, however, require some practice. You will see a lot of free weight exercises in this book and it is a good idea to become familiar with them so you can use more variations.

Basic Techniques

Breathing

Never hold your breath when weight training. This can be dangerous as it causes a build-up of pressure inside your rib cage which can restrict the flow of blood and oxygen to your entire body. As a simple guide to the proper way to breathe, you should inhale when lowering the weight and exhale when lifting the weight. In other words think of 'blowing up the weight'.

Grips

Throughout your weight training you will be using a variety of machines, barbells and dumb-bells. How you hold or grip these bars is partly a matter of personal preference and partly depends on the movement itself, but the main variations are as shown on the right.

- **a** Underhand
- **b** Overhand
- **c** Alternate
- **d** False

For the most part you will be using underhand and overhand grips. The alternate grip is used to lift a bar from one place to another or to hand it to someone. The false grip is a more advanced technique and reduces pressure on forearm tendons because the thumb is not used to grasp the bar or handle.

Using the equipment safely

Having joined the gym, there are a few things you should know about safety and gym etiquette which are equally important not only to yourself but to all those other members using the gym.

Safety is not only important for yourself but for the people around you too, and the following points will help you to be a considerate member of the gym.

a *Underhand*

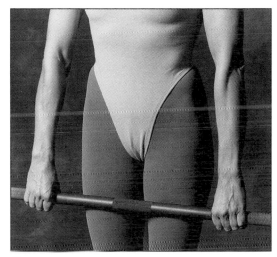

b *Overhand*

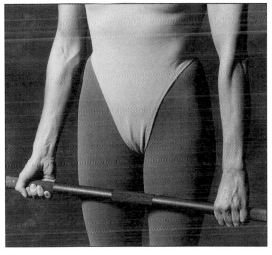

c *Alternate*

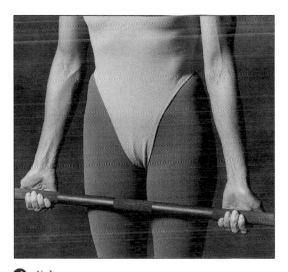

d *False*

1 When you use a machine for the first time, check that the 'pin' for the weight stack is on a light weight. Always use a light weight until you get used to the movement.

2 Every time you use a dumb-bell or barbell for the first time, check that the weights are secure on the dumb-bell or barbell and always use collars to secure the weight properly.

3 Never walk in front of or near another person while they are performing a set as this can interrupt their concentration and could also be dangerous. Wait until they have finished their set.

4 If a particular machine is being used, ask if you can 'work in'. This means that while the other person is resting between their set, you use that machine to do your set. This way neither person has to wait. Conversely, if you are using a machine, always allow a person to 'work in' with you.

Working with a spotter.

Here a spotter helps to take the weight of the barbell.

⑤ You may occasionally be asked to 'spot' someone which means standing behind them while they perform their set and helping them to perform all the reps in the set, or replacing the bar or dumb-bells back on the rack when they finish. 'Spotting' is usually only required by the more experienced weight trainers when they are using heavy weights in awkward positions.

⑥ Always replace your weights on the rack, and remove the plates from the bars after you have finished. This is not only for safety but as a consideration to others training in the gym.

CHAPTER 4

Creating Your Weights Workout

The three components of health and fitness — the three S's — are strength, stamina and suppleness. It is possible be strong, but inflexible, have great stamina but a weak body, be supple but have no strength or stamina. To get a reasonable level of overall fitness, you need all three elements.

For stamina you will need aerobic activity. Aerobic simply means 'with air' and involves any exercise that can be performed continuously for at least twenty minutes, and which increases your heart rate and exercises your lungs. Activities such as jogging, cycling, aerobic dance and fast walking are examples of aerobic exercise. Most of our aerobic work is done on the treadmill.

Cardiovascular workouts

Most gyms have a cardiovascular (CV) section that includes treadmills, bikes, rowers and steppers. We have included photographs of the type of CV equipment you are likely to find, but bear in mind that most of this equipment is computerised nowadays and each will need to be explained by your gym instructor. Any of these CV machines will give you a good cardiovascular workout. Some people use these CV machines as part of their warm-up before beginning their weights workout. Others finish their

Rowing machine.

Treadmill.

Steps.

weight training by spending some time on a CV machine, while others do their CV workout on a different day. It doesn't much matter when you do your cardiovascular workout — before, after or even on a different day to your weights — but you should have warmed up before you start (see page 47). The best way is whichever is the most convenient to you in terms of time and place.

The importance of stretching

As we have said, a weights workout will keep you supple because it pushes the joint through its full range of motion. However, it is still a good idea to include stretches before and after your workout. These help to reduce any muscle soreness, keep the muscles long and toned, and keep your body flexible and supple. See the warm-up routine on page 47.

Get to know your body

Remember that when you exercise, you are working the internal organs as well as strengthening the muscles and joints that surround them. You will become more aware of your body and how it works. As you become more familiar with your weight training exercises, you will begin to feel each muscle group as you exercise it. This is known as the 'feel' or 'technique' referred to on page 45.

As weight training involves working specific muscle groups, it is important to know which muscle group you are exercising. You do not have to know all the technical names and we have included a simple guide with their more common names to the

Know your muscles

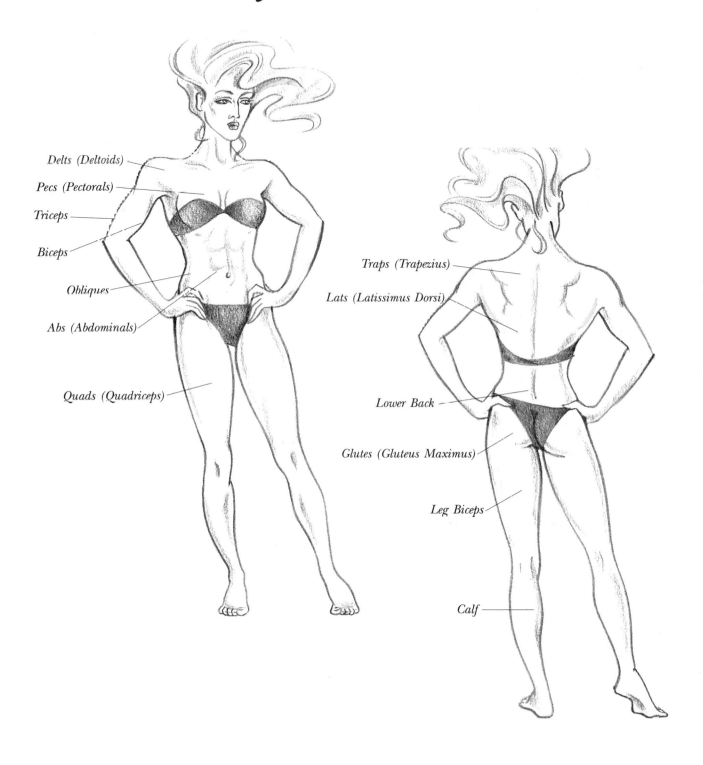

Delts (Deltoids)

Pecs (Pectorals)

Triceps

Biceps

Obliques

Abs (Abdominals)

Quads (Quadriceps)

Traps (Trapezius)

Lats (Latissimus Dorsi)

Lower Back

Glutes (Gluteus Maximus)

Leg Biceps

Calf

muscle groups you will be working. Think of your body as individual parts: shoulders, chest, back, arms (biceps and triceps), abdominals, and legs (thighs, hamstrings and calves). Dividing the body like this will make it easier for you to work out your own programme and to remember which exercises go with each particular body part.

Creating your own routine

Training the whole body in one go is quite strenuous and time-consuming, so it is better to train two body parts in one workout, followed by a day off, and then another two body parts during the next, followed by a day off, and so on, so that the whole body is exercised over two to three sessions a week, allowing for maximum rest and recovery between sessions. This is a day-on, day-off routine. Don't worry if this is not possible — fit the exercise around your life so that you keep up the routine and continue to make progress.

An example is to work the chest and back in one session, the shoulders and arms in another, and the legs in a third. Abdominals can be worked in every session. You could even exercise just one body part if you have a limited amount of time. Although this might mean you make more visits to the gym, your workouts will be shorter.

There are many body part combinations, but the following suggested routines are probably as good as any, and after a time, you will be able to add exercises to suit your own aims. Carolyn has included her own routine as an example, although we stress that this is a more advanced routine and not for the beginner.

This way of 'dividing' the body into parts and exercising one or two body parts per session is known as the split routine as the body is split into parts. Although this way of training is generally considered more advanced, it is a good idea to start your weight training using a basic split routine.

AS AN EXAMPLE, A BASIC BEGINNER'S ROUTINE WOULD BE:

Day 1 Monday or Tuesday Session 1 **Chest and back**

Day 2 Tuesday or Wednesday Rest

Day 3 Wednesday or Thursday Session 2 **Legs**

Day 4 Thursday or Friday Rest

Day 5 Friday or Saturday Session 3 **Shoulders and arms**

Abdominals *can be exercised in each session after your main workout.*

Beginner's routine

This is based on three sessions per week. Do what you can – this is simply a starting point and you can add or subtract exercises as necessary.

Day	Body Part	Exercise	Sets	Reps
1	**Chest**	Bench Press	2-3	10-12
		Dumb-bell Flyes	2-3	10-12
	Back	Lat Pulldown	2-3	10-12
		Low Pulley Row	2-3	10-12
	Abdominals	Crunches	2	15-20
		Reverse Curls	2	15-20
2	**Legs**	Leg Press	2	10-12
		Leg Extension	2	10-12
		Leg Curl	2	10-12
		Calf Raises	2	15-20
	Abdominals	As in Session 1		
3	**Shoulders**	Seated Dumb-bell Press	2	10-12
		Upright Row	2	10-12
	Arms	Bicep Curl	2	10-12
		Tricep Pressdown	2	10-12
	Abdominals	As in Session 1		

Intermediate routine

This is based on three sessions per week.

Day	Body Part	Exercise	Sets	Reps
1	**Chest**	Bench Press	3	10-12
		Incline Press	3	10-12
		Dumb-bell Flyes	3	10-12
	Back	Lat Pulldown	3	10-12
		Low Pulley Row	3	10-12
		Reverse Grip Pulldown	3	10-12
	Abdominals	Crunches	3	15-20
		Oblique Crunches	3	15-20
		Reverse Curls	3	15-20
2	**Legs**	Leg Press	3	10-12
		Leg Extension	3	10-12
		Leg Curl	3	10-12
		Lunges	3	10-12
		Calf Raises	3	10-12
	Abdominals	As in Session 1		
3	**Shoulders**	Seated Dumb-bell Press	3	10-12
		Lateral Raise	3	10-12
		Upright Row	3	10-12
		Bent Over Lateral Raise	3	10-12
	Triceps	Lying Tricep Extension	3	10-12
		Tricep Pushdown	3	10-12
		Kickbacks	3	10-12
	Abdominals	As in Session 1		

Carolyn's advanced routine

This is based on six sessions per week.

Day	Body Part	Exercise	Sets	Reps
1 & 4	Chest	Bench Press	3-4	8-10
		Incline Press	3-4	8-10
		Dumb-bell Flyes	3-4	8-10
		Cable Crossover	3-4	8-10
	Back	Wide Grip Pulldown	3-4	8-10
		Wide Grip In Front	3-4	8-10
		Narrow Reverse Grip In Front	3-4	8-10
		Low Pulley Row	3-4	8-10
		T-Bar Row	3-4	8-10
	Abdominals	Crunches	3	15-20
		Oblique Crunches	3	15-20
		Reverse Curls	3	15-20
		Leg Raises	3	15-20
2 & 5	Legs	Leg Press Regular Foot Position	5-6	8-15
		Leg Press Feet Parallel	2	8-15
		Leg Press Wide Toes Out	2	8-15
		Leg Extension	4-5	10-15
		Leg Curls	4-5	10-15
		Lunges	3-4	10-15
		Stiff Legged Deadlifts	4	10-12
	Calves	Standing Calf Raises	5	15-20
		Seated Calf Raises	5	15-20
	Abdominals	As in Session 1		

Day	Body Part	Exercise	Sets	Reps
3 & 6	**Shoulders and Arms**	Behind The Neck Press	4	8-10
		Upright Rows	3-4	8-10
		Lateral Raises	4	8-10
		Front Raises	4	8-10
		Bent Over Cable Raises	4	8-10
	Triceps	Lying EZ Tricep Extensions	4	8-10
		Tricep Pressdown	4	8-10
		Reverse Grip Pressdown	4	8-10
	Biceps	Standing Barbell Curls	4	8-10
		Seated Alternate Dumb-bell Curls	4	8-10
		Cable Curls	4	8-10
		Preacher Curls	4	8-10
	Abdominals	As in Session 1		

Preparing your workout

Before you go to the gym have some sort of workout routine planned. This will save you time when you are there and ensure that you get the most out of your session.

There are probably more weight training workout routines than there are gyms. Most are either simple variations on a theme or more advanced routines for those who have been training for a number of years. If you are just beginning, stick to the basics and keep it simple.

A lot of what you do will, of course, depend on the amount of time you have and the type of equipment available to you at the gym. As we said earlier, a consistent regular approach will produce the best results. A little and often is the best. If possible, you should try and train at about the same time each day. This way you will develop a routine. If for some reason you have to miss a session, don't worry — there's always another day. If you are new to weight training, a good way to start is the day on, day off routine. This simply means that you work out one day then rest the next day, then work out the next and so on.

Designing your programme

Weight training exercises are performed in what are known as 'sets' and 'reps'. A set is a series of repetitions (reps) of any given exercise. As rule of thumb, do between two and four sets of eight to twelve reps of each exercise. For example, if you perform barbell bicep curls ten times, you will have completed one set which can then be repeated two, three or four times. For optimum results, it is generally accepted that the weight should be lifted for at least eight repetitions, but for no more than 12. However, when you first start, you can use a lighter weight and do a few more repetitions, but no more than 15. Using the 8-12 repetition range, if, with the weight you are using , you can easily continue for more than 12 reps, it is too light. Conversely if, with the weight you are using, you are unable to do at least 8 reps, it is too heavy.

When you begin, limit your workouts to a total of no more than 12 sets per body part. So, when you plan your routine, go for four different exercises of three sets each, three different exercises of four sets each, or even six different exercises of two sets each. Each set should be performed for between eight and ten repetitions. Using our basic body part combination described on page 37, your early workout routine might be as follows. See the exercise chapters for the specific exercises.

Session One — Chest and Back

Either three, four or six different exercises of two to four sets of between eight to ten reps.

Session Two — Shoulders and Arms

Again, either three, four or six different exercises of two three or four sets of between eight to ten reps.

Session Three — Legs

Also either three, four or six different exercises of two, three or four sets of between eight to ten reps.

Abdominals should be done with every workout.

When you first start, try not to wait too long between each set, but rest just long enough to get your breath back — usually about 1-2 minutes. This means you can spend less time in the gym, exercise while your energy levels are high and focus on what you are doing. The longer you rest between sets, the more your body will cool down and the more likely you are to injure yourself.

Having designed a programme, you need to decide which exercises to do for each body part and this will depend on the type of equipment available in your gym and which parts of your body you want to work on. We have shown the basic exercises used in most weight training routines and some variations. Try to use the basic exercises first until you become more familiar with them. Then you can add some of the variations, and design your own personal workout programme.

Weight training should be a gradual progression. Always try for good form and technique, and never try to lift too much weight as this may lead to injury. Do not jerk or swing the weight up or down. Try to make a smooth movement through a full range of motion, and concentrate on the muscle group you are exercising. Start by using a lighter weight but with good form. As you become stronger, you will gradually be able to use a slightly heavier weight.

You should also perform the exercises in a certain order. As a basic rule, do those exercises that involve the larger muscle groups (e.g. the shoulders and legs) and multiple joint movement first. As they require the most energy it is better to do them when your energy level is at its highest. So, work your shoulders before your arms as the shoulders are a large muscle group with multiple joint movement, whereas arms have small muscles and require less energy.

Learning the technique

Weight training does require proper technique and training principles. Learning this technique, which is known as 'the feel', should take no more than three or four months. Without this, your workouts will not be as effective. Time and time again, we have seen women, as well as men, spending hour after hour in the gym with little or no effect. Inevitably this leads to disappointment through lack of progress, with the likely outcome that he or she gives up. In nearly every case the reason for this lack of results is poor technique, using too much or too little weight or a lack of understanding about the exercise being performed. Just a simple understanding of the muscle group being exercised and how the exercise is performed correctl;y makes all the difference. We emphasise the word 'simple' as weight training is not a complicated form of exercise.

CHAPTER 5

Preparing for Your Workout

Before you start to lift weights, there are a few more very important points to remember. We know we said weight training is not complicated, but these points will prevent you from injuring yourself and will help you to make the most of your exercise. They are important, so please take the time to read and understand them. (See also Chapter Three, page 28.)

Raise one arm until horizontal and press across your chest. Repeat with the other arm.

Raise both arms upright. Lower one arm behind your head and clasp the elbow with your other hand. Repeat with the other arm.

Stand with feet slightly apart. Hold onto a suitable piece of equipment with your arm fully extended to the side. Keeping your back straight, twist your upper body slightly away from the extended arm, stretching its full length. Repeat with the other arm.

Warming up

It is always important to warm up properly. This may seem like common sense, but its surprising how many people, including those who have been training for some time, walk into the gym do a few arm swings, then jump on the bench and start pushing heavy weights. If you do this, you will have problems.

A good warm up should last about 5-10 minutes. It can include a few minutes on the stationary bike followed by stretches (see examples shown here), and then a couple of light sets of the first exercise before your main workout. This means that whatever exercise you are going to do first, start off with a very light weight (lighter

Holding onto a piece of equipment, place one leg forward, slightly bent, and stretch out the rear leg. Repeat with the other leg.

Stand with one leg bent and press down on it with your hands. Stretch the other leg forward with the toes flexed. Repeat with the other leg.

than you would normally use) and do a couple of sets to get the muscles used to working. You can also continue to stretch between these sets and throughout your workout. It is also a good idea to stretch the muscles out again after your workout.

Clothing

Comfortable, loose fitting clothing will allow you to move with ease and will keep your body warm between sets. Women often train in a leotard so they can see the muscle being worked and this helps to develop their technique.

Never train in bare feet or sandals as it is both unhygienic and dangerous. A good pair of cross-training shoes is better for weight training than jogging shoes.

Another item you might consider is weight training gloves. These will help you to grip the barbells or dumb-bells better and will also protect your hands.

Always take a towel into the gym with you so you can put it on a bench to keep it clean and so that others do not have to lie on your sweat.

Fluids

Always make sure you take in enough fluid before, during and after your workout. The best fluid replacement is water. Excessive fluid loss through perspiration can diminish your ability to work out. Take a bottle of water into the gym with you so you can drink between sets.

Another option for fluid replacement are sports drinks. There are quite a few on the market today, ranging from simple fluid replacement sports drinks to carbohydrate energy drinks to protein powders. Others are even more specific, claiming to sustain metabolism and inhibit fat storage and even help you to lose or gain weight. We have read many reports on sports drinks, and the general view is that there are as many opinions on the value or otherwise as there are drinks on the market. Our own personal preference when training is to drink water as we find most of these drinks too sweet. If you decide to use a sports drink, read the label carefully. Watch out for those hidden calories. If you still want a drink with taste, you can always dilute a sports drink with water.

Putting it all into practice

We hope that by now you are now filled with enthusiasm and ready to go. As with everything you do in life, it is important to develop a positive attitude. This is true of weight training or of any kind of exercise routine. A regular weight training routine will be extremely helpful in developing a positive approach — in fact one aids the other. A positive attitude when you start will be sustained by your improvements which will encourage you to continue, which in turn will further develop your positive attitude.

Ask yourself what you want to achieve. Be realistic, but set yourself a goal. Give yourself a time frame, where you are today, and where you want to be in, say, three months' time. As you become fitter, stronger and healthier, you will become more confident. This in turn will help you deal with the everyday stresses of modern life.

Remember the only rule in weight training is that there are no rules, and everything changes! There are correct ways to perform an exercise, although even that can be altered to suit a particular person's needs or body type, and there are generally accepted methods of ways to exercise. For best results those new to weight training should, as we've said before, learn the basics. For those of you who have been training for a while, try some of the variations shown in the book.

THE EXERCISES

Each of the following sections is divided into separate body parts for ease of reference. Each exercise is shown in its basic form using machines and free weights, with start and finish positions and with variations. You can use any combination of the exercises for your own programme. It really is up to you. Using weights in your workout puts you in control.

The Ultimate Workout

Remember the key components of your workout:

❶ CV work (as part of warm up)   **❸ Weights exercises**

❷ Stretching   **❹ Stretching (post workout)**

Follow this order and you really will get the most from your time in the gym.

Summary

1 Remember the three 'S' — Strength, Stamina, Suppleness. Include them all in your workouts.

2 Remember the body parts — it will help you understand which part you are exercising.

3 Decide on a training time that you will be able to stick to.

4 Decide on a weight training programme and select your exercises.

5 Learn the proper technique for those exercises and do not try more advanced exercises until you are familiar with the basics.

6 Try to keep a record of your progression.

7 Do not attempt too much when you start.

8 Do not over-train — more is not better.

9 Do not attempt to lift too much weight in certain exercises without a spotter.

10 Always be aware of other people in your gym. It will make for a safer place.

KEY POINTS

Breathing - Exhale on the effort part of the movement.

Good form - Always use good form and control the movement.

Speed - Don't rush the movement.

Repetitions - Perform between 8 and 15 repetitions for each set

CHAPTER 6

THE CHEST

Major Muscles: Pectorals

Secondary Muscles: Triceps/Deltoids

All the exercises in this section will help to shape and firm the muscles which support the bust, improving the cleavage and giving you a better silhouette.

Barbell Bench Press

This is the basic bench press using a free weight Olympic bar. It trains the whole of the chest area and is also known as the chest press.

❶ Take a medium width grip and slowly lower the bar to a point just above your chest.

❷ Slowly press the bar back until your arms are straight.

wide grip

narrow grip

VARIATIONS

As a variation try a wide grip

or a narrow grip. The

movement is the same as the

basic bench press. The varying

hand positions work a slightly

different part of the same

muscle. This exercise can also

be performed on an incline

and decline bench.

Smith Machine

This is the same basic exercise as the bench press only using a smith machine.

❶ If your gym has a smith machine, you will find it is one of the most versatile pieces of

equipment. The main advantage of this machine is that the bar has a self-locking mechanism

which you can use to stop the bar at any point during the movement.

2 It can be used for either flat, incline or decline pressing. Flat pressing works the whole chest, incline exercises the upper chest and decline the lower chest. You will see other uses for the smith machine throughout this book.

Vertical Machine Chest Press

This exercise works the whole chest.

❶ Sit on the seat with your back against the back pad. Press down with your feet on the bar in front. This will bring the handles forward. Grip the handles and remove your feet from the bar.

2 Press slowly outwards and slowly back. Use the foot bar when you have performed the set to take the weight back to the start position.

Incline Machine Chest Press

This is a variation of the vertical machine chest press.

1 Incline pressing works the upper part of the pectoral muscles. Sit on the seat with your back against the back pad. Press down with your feet on the bar in front. This will bring the handles forward. Grip the handles and remove your feet from the bar.

2 Press slowly outwards and slowly back. Use the foot bar when you have performed the set to take the weight back to the start position.

This movement is similar to the vertical chest press except that the movement is at a more upward angle.

Pec Deck

This will help develop the cleavage, exercising the middle area of the chest.

1 This machine also works the chest. The arms are brought together which places more emphasis on the centre of the chest.

2 In this machine the arms start from a wider position, and are then brought together to a position in front of the face.

Dumb-bell Press (Flat)

This is the same movement as the basic barbell press except you use dumb-bells

❶ Lie on a flat bench with the dumb-bells held straight above your chest.

❷ With palms facing forwards and keeping your hands facing forwards, slowly lower the dumb-bells to the side of your chest.

VARIATION

A variation on the dumb-bell

press is to start with the palms

facing inwards and, as you

lower, turn your palms

forwards.

Incline Dumb-bell Press

Incline dumb-bell press is an excellent upper chest exercise giving a fullness in the upper chest and a better silhouette.

❶ Lie on an incline bench and perform the same movements as you would with the previous dumb-bell press, holding dumb-bells straight above your chest.

2 Slowly lower the dumb-bells to the side of your chest, then raise them back to the start position.

Dumb-bell Flyes (Flat)

1 Lie on a flat bench with the dumb-bells pressed over your chest, palms facing inwards.

2 Keep the elbows slightly bent throughout the movement and slowly lower the dumb-bells out to each side. Bring the dumb-bells back to the start position.

Dumb-bell Flyes (cont)

As a variation this exercise can also be performed on an incline bench.

❶ Lie on a incline bench with the dumb-bells pressed over your chest, palms facing inwards.

❷ Keep the elbows slightly bent throughout the movement and slowly lower the dumb-bells out to each side. Bring the dumb-bells back to the start position.

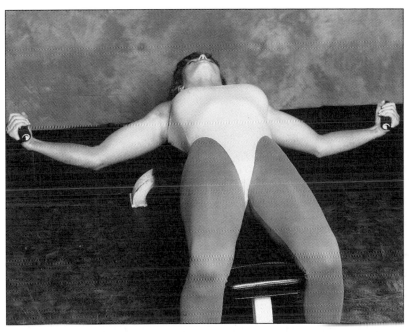

VARIATION

Another more advanced variation is to perform this exercise using the cable cross over machine. Your technique needs to be good to use the cables, so this variation is far the more advanced.

Dumb-bell Pullover

These are more difficult exercises and should only be attempted when you have a spotter to assist you.

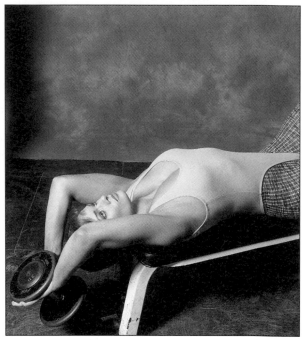

❶ Lie on a flat bench and hold a single dumb-bell with both hands above the head.

❷ Slowly lower the dumb-bell behind the head, allowing the arms to bend at the lower part of the movement. Pull the dumb-bell up over the head to the start position.

VARIATIONS

A variation of the dumb-bell

pullover is to use a straight bar.

(See left)

An advanced variation is to lie

across the bench with feet on

the floor and shoulder blades

touching the bench. The hips

are low and the dumb-bell is

lowered as opposite.

Cable Crossover

This is very good at developing the central part of the chest, bringing fullness and a more developed cleavage. Cables are an excellent shaping exercise, needing a moderate to light weight.

❶ Stand in the centre of the cables and grasp a handle in each hand. Step forwards so that the arms are outstretched.

❷ Keeping your arms slightly bent, pull the arms together to a position in front of your chest.

VARIATION

As a variation, try bringing your

hands to a lower position and

crossing your hands over.

Dips

This is a very difficult exercise and should not be performed until you are relatively experienced. You may need a spotter to take the weight of your legs, even if you are quite strong.

❶ Position yourself on a dipping station with your arms straight and with the body leaning slightly forwards.

2 Slowly lower yourself until your arms are parallel with the bars, then push yourself up until your arms are straight.

KEY POINTS

Breathing - Exhale on the effort part of the movement.

Good form - Always use good form and control the movement.

Speed - Don't rush the movement.

Repetitions - Perform between 8 and 15 repetitions for each set.

CHAPTER 7

THE BACK

Major Muscles: Latissimus Dorsi

Secondary Muscles: Rhomboids/Rear

Deltoids/Biceps

These exercises will help to give you a toned and shapely back, as well as strengthening and supporting the vertebrae, helping to prevent injury and improve posture.

Lat Pulldown

This is one of the main exercises for shaping the back.

❶ Grasp the bar with a fairly wide hand grip and sit on the seat facing the machine with your knees secured under the knee pads.

❷ With a steady, even movement, pull the bar down to a position just above your neck.

VARIATION

A variation of this exercise is

to pull the bar down to a

position in front of the chest.

When doing this movement

you should keep the back

slightly arched and the chest

up **(a, b)**.

3 Then, also with control, allow the bar to return to the start position. Try not to let the weight touch the stack, thereby keeping tension on the back muscles at all times.

a

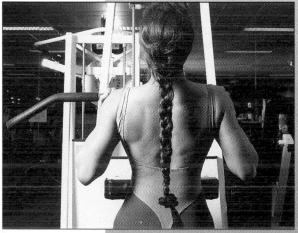

b

Seated Machine Vertical Row

This exercise works the upper middle back rear deltroids and rhomboids.

❶ Sit facing the machine and grip the handles with arms fully extended.

2 Pull both handles back as far possible. Slowly return to the start position.

Low Pulley Row

This exercise works the upper and middle back.

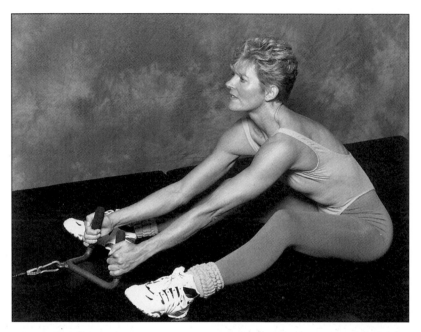

❶ Either use a cable machine as shown here or a low pulley row machine. Sit on the seat and place both feet slightly apart on the footplate. Keep your knees slightly bent.

❷ Grasp the handle with both hands and with a steady movement pull the handle in to a position just below your chest. Keep your elbows back and your chest high.

a

b

c

d

VARIATIONS

A variation is the single arm cable row using the cable crossover machine with a handle attached to the lower position of the weight stack **(a, b)**.

Another more advanced exercise using the cable crossover is the straight arm pressdown. Grasp the short bar on the cable machine with your arms extended and knees bent **(c)**. Keeping your arms straight, press the bar down **(d)**.

T-bar Rowing

This is an advanced exercise which works the whole back. Do not attempt it if you have any back injuries.

❶ Stand with your feet either side of the bar. Keeping your back straight, bend forwards and grasp the handle of the T-bar.

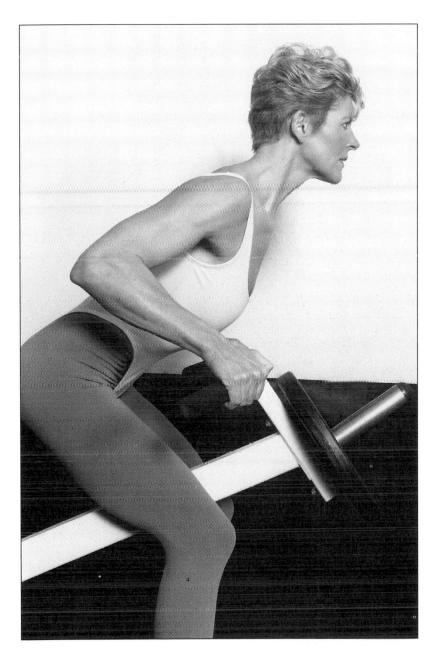

2 Pull the bar upwards into your body keeping your elbows back and to your sides. Keep your knees slightly bent and do not round your back.

Bent Over Barbell Rowing

This exercise is good for the whole back but is advanced.

❶ Stand with your knees slightly bent and grasp a barbell with your hands slightly wider than shoulder width.

❷ Keeping your knees bent and your back straight, pull the bar into a position just above your waist. Lower the bar back to the start position.

VARIATION

An easier variation of the bent

over barbell row is the single

arm dumb-bell row.

Chins

This is a difficult exercise and should not be performed until you are very advanced and have developed good upper body strength. Work with a spotter the first time you try this.

❶ Take a wide grip on the chinning bar and pull yourself up until your chin is level with the bar.

2 Slowly, and with control, lower yourself back to the start position.

KEY POINTS

Breathing - Exhale on the effort part of the movement.

Good form - Always use good form and control the movement.

Speed - Don't rush the movement.

Repetitions - Perform between 8 and 15 repetitions for each set.

CHAPTER 8

THE SHOULDERS

Major Muscles: Trapezius/Deltoids

Secondary Muscles: Biceps/Triceps

These exercises will help to improve your posture and to give a shapely, defined look to the shoulders. Well toned shoulders will make your clothes fit and hang better, while their broadness will make your waist appear smaller.

Seated Machine Press

This is a basic movement which works the deltoid area.

❶ Sit with your back against the back pad and grasp the handles which should be at shoulder height, with your palms facing forwards.

2 Press the handles straight up above your head and slowly lower back to the start position. Some machines will have various hand positions, e.g. palms facing inwards.

Seated Dumb-bell Press

This is another good, basic exercise, creating shapely shoulders.

❶ As an alternative to the seated machine press, this exercise can be performed with dumb-bells. Sit on an adjustable bench with the back in the upright position. Start with the dumb-bells held at shoulder height, palms facing forwards.

❷ Press the dumb-bells straight up above your head and slowly lower them to the start position.

VARIATIONS

A variation is the ALTERNATE

DUMB-BELL PRESS which can

be done either seated or

standing. In this exercise only

one dumb-bell is pressed at a

time.

Smith Machine Press behind the Neck

This is a basic exercise.

❶ Sit on an adjustable bench with the back upright and with the bar behind your neck.

❷ With a grip slightly wider than shoulder width, press the

bar straight up. Slowly lower the bar to the start position.

Press Behind The Neck

❶ A variation of this is the PRESS BEHIND THE NECK using a barbell. As this is a difficult exercise it may be advisable to use a spotter.

Seated Machine Deltoid Raise

This exercise works the side deltoid, defining the shoulders and the tops of the arms.

❶ Sit facing the machine with your arms bent and grasp the handles. The outer pad will be against your upper arm.

2 Raise your elbows out to the side until they are level with your shoulder and slowly lower the weight back to the start position.

Standing Dumb-bell Lateral Raise

This is the same as the previous exercise but instead uses free weights.

❶ Hold the dumb-bells in front, palms facing each other.

❷ Slowly raise the dumb-bells to a position just above your shoulders, then slowly lower the dumb-bells back to the start position.

This exercise can be performed either standing or seated on a bench, as shown above.

Standing Single Arm Dumb-bell Lateral Raise

The same as the standing dumb-bell lateral raise, one side is worked at a time enabling a heavier weight to be used.

❶ It is recommended that you hold on to a solid piece of equipment while performing this exercise. Hold the dumb-bell in front of you.

❷ Slowly raise the dumb-bell to just above your shoulder, then slowly lower back to the start position.

VARIATION

A variation of this exercise is

the SINGLE ARM CABLE

LATERAL RAISE. This involves

the same movement as the

previous exercise except uses

the cable crossover machine.

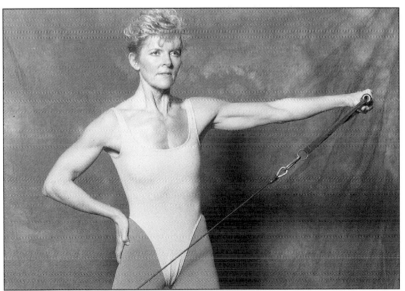

Front Dumb-bell Raise

As the deltoids have three parts - front, side and rear - it is important to work all the parts. The side lateral raise exercises the side deltoid muscle, while the front raise exercises the front deltoid muscle.

❶ Hold a pair of dumb-bells in front of your thighs, palms towards your body, and keep the arms straight.

❷ Slowly raise the dumb-bells to shoulder level, then slowly lower them back to the start position.

VARIATION

This exercise can also be

performed using a barbell, but

this variation is very difficult.

Alternate Front Dumb-bell Raise

Concentrate on each arm, with this basic front deltoid exercise.

❶ This is the same as the front dumb-bell raise except only one arm is raised at a time. Start in the same position.

❷ Raise one arm, then lower to the start position. Repeat with the other arm.

VARIATION

This exercise can also be performed using the

cable crossover machine.

Bent Over Lateral Raise

This exercise works the rear deltoids to give a well balanced look to the shoulders.

❶ Sit on the end of a bench with the dumb-bells held behind your legs with your upper body bent forwards.

❷ Slowly raise the dumb-bells out to the side to the level of your shoulders, then slowly lower them to the start position.

VARIATION

This exercise can also be performed standing.

Bent Over Lateral Raise

VARIATION

For a variation of this exercise, you can use the cable crossover machine, with either alternate arm movements **(a, b)** or simultaneaus arm movements **(c,d)**.

A more advanced variation is to perform this exercise using an adjustable incline bench. **(e,f)**.

a

b

c

d

e

f

Upright Rowing (Barbell)

This exercise works the trapezius and front deltoids, giving a nice 'tie in' between the biceps and deltoids.

❶ Hold the barbell in an overhand grip with the hands approximately 20-25 cm (8-10 in) apart. Lift the bar to a position just below your chin.

❷ Allow your elbows to come up and out during the movement. Slowly lower the bar back to the start position. Pull back slightly to work the deltoid and back as well.

a

VARIATIONS

This exercise can also be performed using

dumb-bells **(a)**.

Another variation is to use a straight bar with the

cable crossover machine. **(b, c)**.

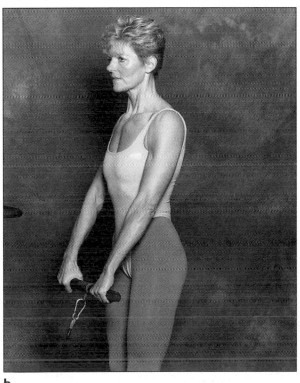

b

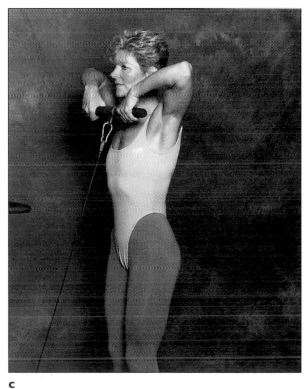

c

Shrugs

This exercise requires relatively heavy dumb-bells. It helps to build up the trapezius by using very small movements.

❶ Take a dumb-bell in each hand with your arms straight down by your sides. Keeping your arms straight, raise the shoulders up and down as in a 'shrug'.

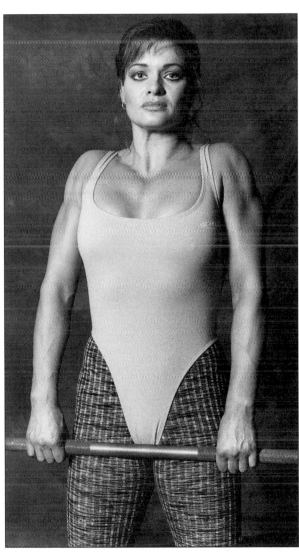

❷ This exercise can also be performed using a barbell or smith machine.

KEY POINTS

Breathing - Exhale on the effort part of the movement.

Good form - Always use good form and control the movement.

Speed - Don't rush the movement.

Repetitions - Perform between 8 and 15 repetitions for each set

CHAPTER 9

THE LEGS

Major Muscles: Gluteus Maximus/Quadriceps

Hamstrings/Calves

As the leg muscles are the largest muscle group in the body and are used so much in everyday activities, they require more exercise and a greater variety. These exercises will help to tone and shape the legs and glutes, and also prevent a build-up of cellulite.

45 Degree Leg Press

This is one of the main exercises for overall leg development

1 Sit with your back firmly supported on the back rest, legs straight, and place both feet on the footplate approximately 30-38 cm (12-15 in) apart.

2 Slowly bend your knees, and lower the weight until your knees are fully bent, then push the weight back again until your legs are straight.

narrow

wide

VARIATION

A variation is to use both

narrow and wide feet

positions. The narrow position

works the outer thigh while

the wide position exercises the

inner thigh.

Lying Machine Leg Press

These machines work by straightening the legs and pushing the body back.

❶ Lie on the machine with your knees bent, and hold onto the handles.

2 Push with your legs until they are straight. Slowly bend your knees back to the start position.

Barbell Squats

This is an advanced exercise for the front of the thighs and bottom. It is not for everyone because of the inherent injury potential to knees and vertebrae. It does require a certain amount of technique and should not be attempted without a 'spotter'.

❶ Start from a standing position with a barbell on your shoulders and grasp the barbell with both hands, feet about shoulder-width apart. Keep your back straight throughout the movement..

❷ Slowly bend your knees until your thighs are parallel with the floor. Do not bend too far forwards. As you reach the parallel position, push up using your thighs to reach the start position. Do not 'bounce' at the bottom of the movement.

narrow

wide

If you are training on your own, you can perform this exercise using the smith machine instead of a barbell.

VARIATION

As with the 45 degree leg press, you can use different feet positions for the squat. This wide stance variation is good for the inner thigh.

Barbell Squats (variations)

An advanced variation is the FRONT SQUAT. Place
a barbell across your shoulders in front.

Grasp the bar by crossing both arms. Keep your
elbows up.

Another variation on the squat is WIDE LEG
SQUAT using a dumb-bell or barbell.

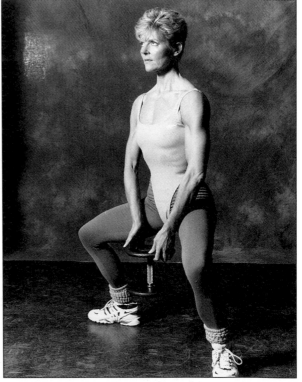

Hold a dumb-bell with both hands in front and take
a wide foot position.

Another variation is to perform the squat using only your body weight **(a, b, c)**.

a

b

c

Another variation on the free standing squat is to take either a narrow foot position or wide foot position and, while holding on to a secure piece of equipment, perform the squat exercise. **(d, e)**.

d

e

Sissy Squats

This is an isolation exercise that specifically works the front of the thighs.

❶ Stand with your feet parallel and hold on to a secure piece of equipment.

2 Raise yourself up on to your toes and perform a squat movement but keeping your hips pushed forwards. Do not completely straighten your legs at the top of the movement, but keep them slightly bent in order to keep tension in the thighs.

Hack Squat

This is a more advanced exercise and is good for the front of the thighs.

❶ Place both feet on the footplate, and grasp the handles with both hands. The handles on a hack squat machine are used to 'unlock' the mechanism.

❷ Keeping your back firmly against the back pad, slowly bend you knees until they are almost parallel. Slowly straighten your legs to the start position. As with squat, do not bounce at the bottom of the movement.

Leg Extension

This is a good basic exercise which helps to create definition to the front of the thighs.

1 Sit on the seat and tuck both feet behind the 'roller pads'. Grasp the handles.

2 Keeping your feet flexed, raise your legs up until they are fully straight. Try to hold this position for a second and slowly lower them back to the start position. Make sure you only use your quadriceps to lift the weight. Do not swing your legs or let the weight drop back. Lift and lower the weight slowly and smoothly under control.

Lying Machine Leg Curl

This exercise helps to tighten and shape the hamstrings and glutes.

❶ Lie face down and tuck both feet under the 'roller pads', and grasp the handles..

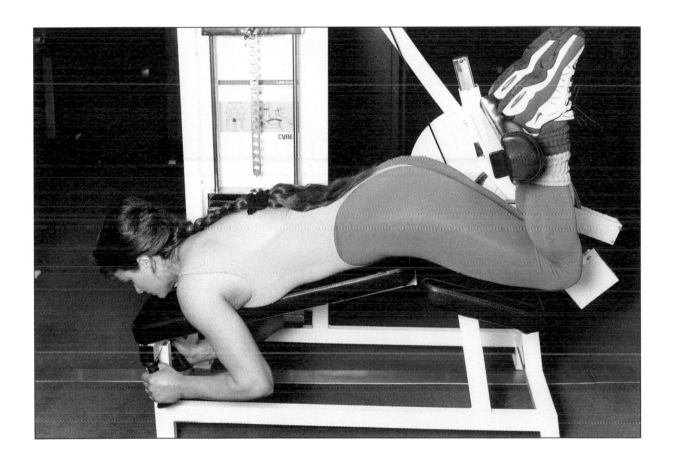

❷ Curl both legs back until the roller pads touch the back of your legs. Make sure you bring the legs back using only the hamstrings. Keep your body flat on the bench and do not swing the weight up or lct it drop down. Lift and lower the weight under control.

Seated Machine

This is a variation of the lying leg curl. This is a good machine to use if you have back problems.

❶ Sit with your knees under the knee pad, and your legs extended.

❷ Pull your feet downwards and back. Slowly straighten your legs to the start position.

VARIATION

A variation on the leg curl is to use the lower attachment on the cable crossover. Attach the ankle strap, stand facing the weight stack and curl your leg back.

Lunges (using a Barbell)

All the lunges shown here are excellent for the glutes, hamstrings and quadriceps.

❶ Start from a standing position with a barbell placed across your shoulders.

❷ Take a long step forward and bend the knee until your thigh is parallel with the floor. Step back to the start position and make the exact same movement with the other leg. Step back to the start position.

a

b

c

d   e

VARIATIONS

One variation is to perform this

exercise to the side. As with

the previous exercise, step to

the side and do 8-15

repetitions, first with one leg

and then change to the other

(a).

Another variation is to perform

both these exercises using

dumb-bells **(b, c)**.

A third variation is to step

forward with your foot on to a

box **(d, e)**.

Step Ups
(using a Barbell)

This exercise is great for the glutes. The higher the step, the harder the exercise.

❶ Start from a standing position with a barbell across your shoulders.

❷ Step up on to a box and then step back to the start position.

❸ Repeat the movement with the other

leg.

VARIATION

Another variation is to perform this exercise

using dumb-bells.

Cable Kickbacks

This is a key exercise for lifting the glutes.

❶ Attach an ankle strap to your ankle. Clip the strap to the lower cable on the crossover machine and, holding the handles, face the weight stack.

❷ Flex your foot and, keeping your leg straight, lift and pull your leg backwards. Make sure you do not arch your back.

VARIATIONS

A variation is to place one knee on a flat bench and raise the leg up and back **(a, b).**

a

b

Adductors

This exercise tones the inner thigh.

❶ Attach the ankle strap on the cable crossover with your leg and extend out to the side.

2 Keeping your leg straight, pull your leg across and in front of your supporting leg.

Good Mornings

This exercise works the bottom and hamstrings and also benefits the lower back.

❶ Start from a standing position with a barbell across your shoulders.

2 Keeping your back straight and head up, slowly bend forwards until your upper body is almost parallel to the floor. Slowly straighten up to the start position.

Stiff Legged Deadlift

This exercise is great for the lower back, glutes and hamstrings. It also gives the hamstrings an added stretch.

❶ Start from a standing position on a secure box or bench with a barbell held in front of your thighs.

2 Keeping your back straight and head up, slowly bend forwards and lower the bar towards the floor. Slowly straighten up to the start position.

Standing Machine Calf Raise

This is an isolation exercise which will help to develop shapely calves.

❶ Stand with your shoulders under the shoulder pads with your legs straight.

❷ Raise your heels up and down again.

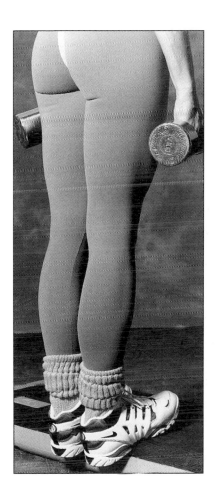

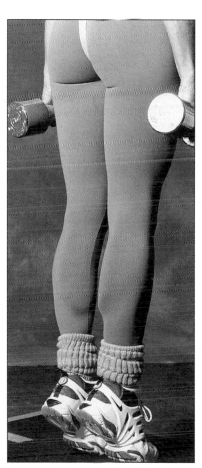

VARIATION

A variation of the machine calf

raise is to use dumb-bells on a

low box or step.

Seated Calf Raise

This exercise isolates the lower calf.

1 Sit with your knees under the knee pads.

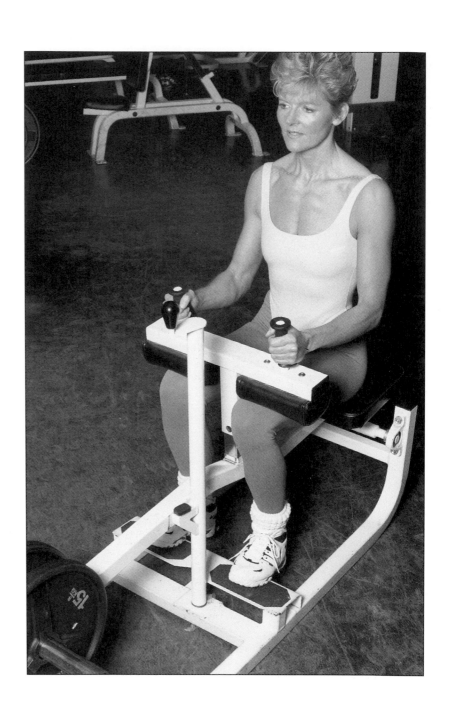

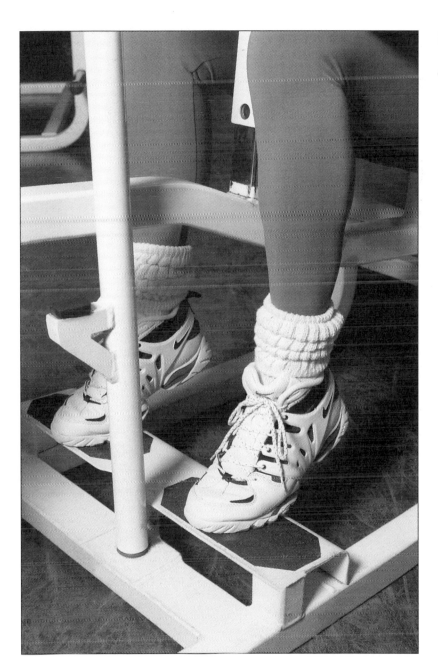

2 Raise your heels up and down.

KEY POINTS

Breathing - Exhale on the effort part of the movement.

Good form - Always use good form and control the movement.

Speed - Don't rush the movement.

Repetitions - Perform between 8 and 15 repetitions for each set.

CHAPTER 10

THE ARMS

Major Muscle: Biceps/Triceps

It is essential to include arm exercises in your routine to give a balanced look to your body and to help keep the backs of the arms toned and sleek.

Seated Arm Curl Machine

This exercise works the bicep muscles.

❶ Sit on the seat and grasp both handles, arms extended in front with your elbows resting on the pads.

❷ Curl your arms up and back towards your face, keeping your elbows on the pads. Slowly allow your arms to straighten back to the start position.

Standing Barbell Curl

This is a basic exercise which works the whole bicep area, building shape and definition. When using free weights, try to perform the exercises through a full range of movement.

❶ Take an underhand grip slightly wider than shoulder width, with your arms straight.

2 Curl the bar up towards your shoulders. Try to keep your elbows close to your sides and do not let them come forwards. Slowly lower the bar back to the start position.

Standing Barbell Curl

a

b

c

d

e

f

VARIATIONS

As a variation, this exercise can also be performed using an EZ Curl Ba.r **(a, b)**.

Another variation of the standing bicep curl is the BICEP CABLE CURL. This is the same exercise as the standing barbell curl except you use the cable crossover machine **(c, d)**.

A third variation of the bicep cable curl is the SINGLE ARM CABLE CURL **(e, f)**.

Standing Alternate Dumb-bell Curl

This is another basic exercise which is good for the biceps.

❶ From a standing position hold a dumb-bell in each hand, arms straight to your sides and palms facing in.

2 Slowly curl one dumb-bell to your shoulder.

3 Slowly lower to the start position and repeat with your other arm.

a

b

VARIATION

As a variation you can curl both arms simultaneously **(a, b)**.

Seated Alternate Dumb-bell Curl

① This is another variation on the standing dumb-bell curl.

VARIATION

This can also be performed using both arms

simultaneously.

Incline Alternate Dumb-bell Curl

❶ As a more advanced exercise of the seated dumb-bell curl, you can use an incline bench and perform either alternate curls or work both arms simultaneously.

Preacher Curl

This exercise uses a Preacher bench and EZ bar. It gives a 'peak' or rise to the centre of the bicep.

❶ Take a narrow underhand grip on the EZ Bar.

❷ Keep your elbows against the bench and curl the bar up towards your shoulders. remember to squeeze at the top of the movement. Try not to let your elbows move outwards and keep your wrists straight throughout the movement. Slowly lower the bar back to the start position.

Concentration Curl

This is an isolation exercise.

❶ Take a dumb-bell in one hand and sit on a bench. Your arm should be straight with your upper arm resting against the inside of your knee.

❷ Without moving your elbow away from your knee, slowly curl the dumb-bell up towards your shoulder. Slowly lower the dumb-bell back to the start position.

Seated Tricep Machine

This machine exercise isolates the triceps very effectively.

❶ Grasp both handles with your elbows resting on the pads.

❷ Keeping your elbows firmly in place, slowly extend your arms and return to the start position.

Tricep Pressdown

This is a good, basic exercise.

 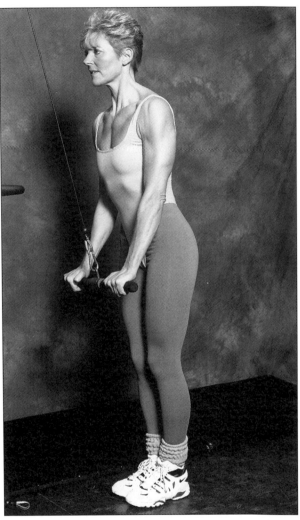

❶ Grasp with the bar with both hands, elbows into your sides.

❷ Slowly press the bar down until your arms are fully extended. Slowly and with control allow the bar to return to the start position. Try not to let your elbows move forwards throughout the movement.

VARIATION

An advanced variation of this exercise is to start

with your back to the weight stack, leaning

forwards with your arms high. Keep your elbows

in line with your body as you straighten your

arms.

Lying Tricep Extension

This is a more advanced exercise and for safety it is best to have a spotter to hand you the bar.

❶ Lying on a flat bench, take a narrow grip on the EZ bar, arms extended. Slowly bend your arms until the bar is at a position just above your forehead.

2 Slowly straighten your arms until they are back to the start position. Try not to let your elbows move out or back throughout the movement.

Seated Tricep Extension using Dumb-bell

❶ Hold a dumb-bell with both hands above your head, arms fully extended.

❷ Slowly lower the dumb-bell behind your head. Try not to let your arms move too far back. Slowly extend your arms back to the start position.

VARIATION

A variation of this exercise is the

SINGLE ARM DUMB-BELL EXTENSION.

Kickbacks

For this exercise you can either support yourself with one hand on your thigh or by placing one knee on a bench. This is good for definition.

❶ Hold a dumb-bell in one hand with your upper arm parallel to the floor.

2 Slowly extend your arm backwards. Slowly bring the weight back to the start position. Do not swing the weight from your shoulder or allow your elbow to move up or down.

Reverse Grip Tricep Pulldown

This exercise is similar to the tricep pressdown

❶ Bend slightly forward and take an underhand grip.

❷ Keeping the elbows in position, slowly extend the arms downwards. Slowly allow the weight back to the start position.

a

b

c

d

VARIATIONS

As a variation this exercise can

also be performed using one

arm at a time either facing,

(a, b) or side-on to the

weight stack **(c, d)**.

Dips

Try to keep your body in the exact position shown in the photographs when performing this exercise.

❶ Take a position with your hands firmly placed on the edge of a bench. Slowly bend your arms to lower your body towards the floor.

❷ Straighten your arms and raise your body back to the start position. Try not to let your elbows move out to the side during the movement.

a

b

c

d

VARIATIONS

An intermediate variation is to perform this exercise between two benches **(a, b)**.

Another advanced and more difficult variation is to perform the exercise using a DIPPING STATION **(c, d)**.

KEY POINTS

Breathing - Exhale on the effort part of the movement.

Good form - Always use good form and control the movement.

Speed - Don't rush the movement.

Repetitions - Perform between 15 and 25 repetitions for each set.

CHAPTER 11

THE ABDOMINALS

Major Muscle: Rectus Abdominus/Obliques

A flat stomach is what every woman wants. Strong abdominal muscles help to protect the back and internal organs. A well toned mid-section creates a pleasing and aesthetic look.

Seated Abdominal Machine

❶ Sit with the pads against your upper body.

2 Slowly curl yourself forwards and then back to the start position.

Crunch

This exercise can be done either on a bench or on the floor.

❶ Lie with your back flat and your knees bent, your head supported by your hands.

2 Without arching your back, slowly raise your shoulders. Try not to allow your shoulders to touch the floor or bench on the downward movement, and not to let your head come too far forwards.

Oblique Crunch

This is similar to the crunch exercise and works the muscles on the side of the waist.

1 Starting from the same position but with one foot resting on the opposite knee, raise your shoulders and twist your body towards the knee. Slowly lower and repeat with the other knee.

Sit Ups

Use a sit-up board or a bench with your feet secured by a spotter. This exercise works the whole of the abdominals.

❶ Curl your body upwards towards your knees, keeping your arms forwards. Slowly lower yourself back to the start position.

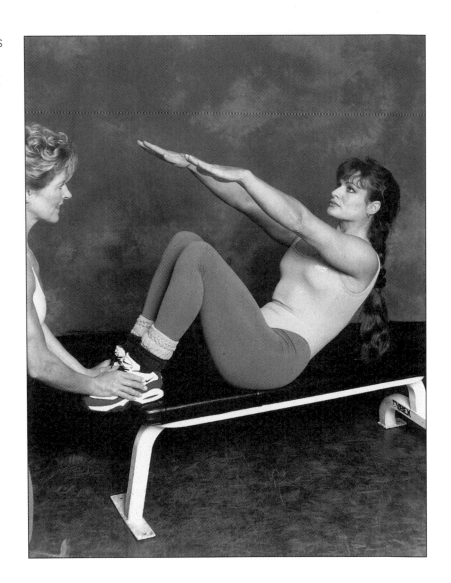

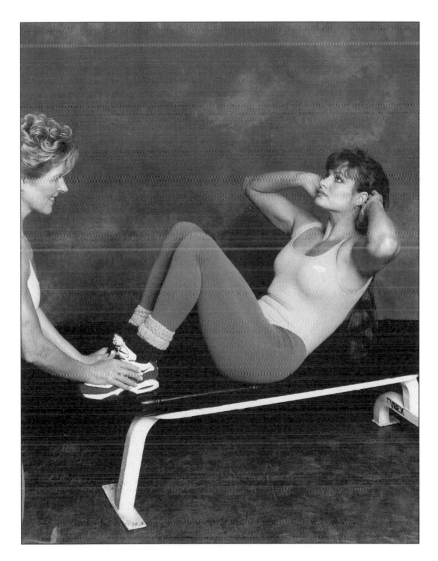

❷ A more advanced variation is to place your hands behind your head.

Reverse Curl

This exercise places more stress on the lower abdominal section.

❶ Lie on your back with your feet off the floor and knees bent. Keep your hands under your hips.

2 Raise your hips up and towards your chest, and lower under control.

Leg Raise

This is an advanced exercise and should only be performed once you have achieved good abdominal strength.

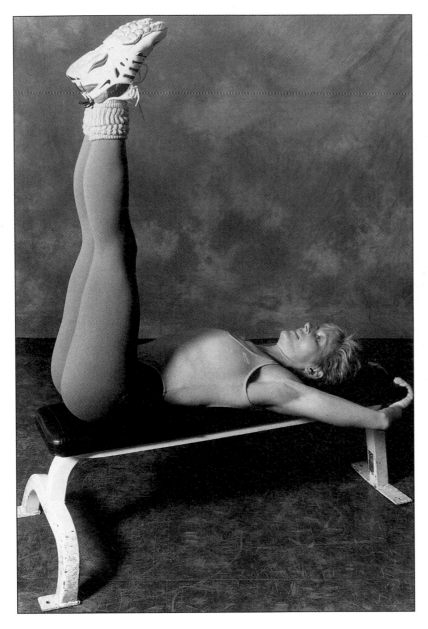

❶ Lie on a bench and raise your legs up and down.

2 Try not to arch your back but concentrate the movement in your abdominal muscles.

Hanging Knee Raise

This is a very advanced exercise which is particularly good for the lower abdominal area.

❶ This is another advanced abdominal exercise which requires not only abdominal strength but good upper body strength as well.

❷ It is important not to let your body swing forward and back throughout the movement. Keep your knees together as you raise your legs.

VARIATION

Another advanced variation is

to keep the legs straight.

Glossary of Common Gym Terms

ABS - abbreviation for abdominals.

AEROBIC EXERCISE - continuous activity of a modest intensity.

BARBELL - a long steel bar 1.2-2-7 m (4-9 feet) in length with either fixed or adjustable weights at either end.

BENCHES - basic benches used for a variety of exercises using either dumb-bells or barbells. Benches are either flat, incline, decline or adjustable from flat to incline.

BI'S and TRI'S - abbreviation for biceps and triceps.

BURN - a feeling in the muscle when it has been pushed to its limits.

CHEATING - to use other muscle groups apart than those being exercised to assist in the movement. Usually associated with using too much weight.

COLLAR - a clamp or device used to secure the weights on dumb-bells or barbells.

DUMB-BELL - shorter version of a barbell, also with fixed or adjustable weights at each end.

EZ BAR - an irregular shaped bar used for curling exercises as it removes strain from the wrists.

PLATE - a circular weight placed on either end of a barbell or dumb-bell. It comes in various weights from light to heavy.

PUMP - this term is used to describe the feeling in a muscle when it is filled with blood.

REP - a repetition is a single movement of an exercise.

ROUTINE - a training programme or schedule.

SET - a number of repetitions of a particular exercise.

SMITH MACHINE - a special type of exercise machine where the bar that moves up and down on guide rods can be locked in several places by rotating the bar and locking it in position.

SPLIT ROUTINE - to exercise certain body parts on one day and other body parts on another rather than exercising the whole body.

SPOTTER - a person who assists another in performing their set in case of difficulty.

SUPER SETS - alternating exercises of one particular muscle group and then immediately moving onto another muscle group in one continuous set.

SUPPLEMENTS - vitamins, minerals and proteins that are used to supplement the diet.

TRAINING PARTNER - a person who regularly trains with another doing the same programme.

TRI SETS - alternating exercise between three muscle groups in one continuous set.

WARM-UP - the first 5-10 minute session before the start of the actual weight training session.

Acknowledgements

We would like to thank the following people for their generous help and support:

Hot Skins leotards supplied by UK Bodywear Ltd (01384 444055)

Espree Fitness, Royal Mint Court and Blackfriars

Pat Wallace, Polaroid UK

Richard Kirkwood, City Camera Exchange

David Montague, Sloane Square Clinic

Michael Wendrow, chiropractor

John Mifsud, McMillan & Co

Premier Health & Fitness Club

Lizzie Welch

Caroline Davidson Literary Agency

Index